CHARLES DARWIN
On the trail of evolution

Clint Twist

Evans Brothers Limited

Evans Brothers Limited
2A Portman Mansions
Chiltern Street
London W1M 1LE

Printed in Hong Kong

ISBN 0 237 51264 5

Series editor: Su Swallow
Editor: Nicola Barber
Designer: Neil Sayer
Production: Peter Thompson

Maps and Illustrations: Brian Watson, Linden Artists

Acknowledgements

For permission to reproduce copyright material the author and
publishers gratefully acknowledge the following:

Cover (top left) rainforest flower — Stephen Dalton, NHPA,
(top middle) 19th-century illustrations of beetles — Derrick
Whitty, Robert Harding Picture Library, (top right) hand axe —
The Natural History Museum, London, (bottom left) marine
iguana — Trevor McDonald, NHPA, (bottom right) giant tortoise
— Haroldo Palo, NHPA.
Title page The Natural History Museum, London.
page 4 (top) reproduced by courtesy of the Royal College of
Surgeons of England, Rainbird, Robert Harding Picture Library
(bottom) Mary Evans Picture Library **page 5** Jany Sauvanet,
NHPA **page 6** Mary Evans Picture Library **page 7** Robert
Harding Picture Library **page 8** Mary Evans Picture Library
page 9 Mary Evans Picture Library **page 10** Mary Evans Picture
Library **page 11** (top) Mary Evans Picture Library, (bottom) e.t.
archive **page 12** Mary Evans Picture Library **page 13** National
Library of Medicine, Science Photo Library **page 14** National
Maritime Museum **page 15** Mary Evans Picture Library **page 16**
National Maritime Museum, e.t. archive **page 17** Frans Lauting.
Bruce Coleman Limited **page 18** (top) National Maritime
Museum, Rainbird, Robert Harding Picture Library, (bottom)
Rainbird, Robert Harding Picture Library **page 19** (top) David
Woodfall, NHPA, (bottom) Tony Craddock, Science Photo
Library **page 20** Robert Harding Picture Library **page 21** (top)
Haroldo Palo, NHPA, (middle) James Carmichael Jr., NHPA,
(bottom) Stephen Dalton, NHPA **page 22** (top) Mary Evans
Picture Library, (bottom) G.I. Bernard, NHPA **page 23** (top)
Rainbird, Robert Harding Picture Library, (bottom) M.P. Kahl,
Bruce Coleman Limited **page 24** Konrad Wothe, Bruce
Coleman Limited **page 25** (top) Philippa Scott, NHPA,
(middle) Dieter & Mary Plage, Bruce Coleman Limited,
(bottom) Bill Paton, NHPA **page 26** (top) Nicholas Devore III,
Bruce Coleman Limited, (middle) The Natural History Museum,
London, (bottom) E.A. Janes, NHPA **page 27** Darwin Museum,
Down House **page 28** Mary Evans Picture Library **page 29**
Mary Evans Picture Library **page 30** (top) The Natural History
Museum, London, (bottom) Jane Burton, Bruce Coleman
Limited **page 32** Haroldo Palo, NHPA **page 33** Frans Lanting,
Bruce Coleman Limited **page 34** Stephen Krasemann, NHPA
page 35 The Illustrated London News Picture Library **page 36**
Mary Evans Picture Library **page 37** The Illustrated London
News Picture Library **page 38** (top) CNRI, Science Photo
Library, (bottom) Sinclair Stammers, Science Photo Library
page 39 (top) Daniel Heuclin, NHPA, (bottom) Jim Amos,
Science Photo Library **page 41** Chemical Design Ltd, Science
Photo Library **page 42** (top) The Natural History Museum,
London (bottom) F Jacain, Robert Harding Picture Library
page 43 John Reader, Science Photo Library.

Contents

Introduction

Charles Darwin was a young man only 22 years old when he set out on his five-year voyage around the world.

In 1836, the English naturalist Charles Darwin returned from a five-year, round-the-world voyage aboard the survey ship, *HMS Beagle*. His job on the voyage had been to collect plants, animals, fossils and minerals from all over the world. On his return, Darwin began to develop a theory of evolution based on his own observations, and influenced by certain other scientists and writers. When Darwin's theory of evolution was finally published, more than 20 years later, it caused a great public outcry. Yet, within a few years, his theory had become generally accepted.

This book tells the story of Charles Darwin and his theory of evolution. The book also shows how other scientists, before and after Darwin, have contributed to our understanding of the natural world.

A voyage of adventure

The voyage of the *Beagle* was an amazing adventure for Charles Darwin. The young man who had never before made a journey of more than 500 kilometres sailed around the world, covering a

HMS Beagle, Darwin's home for almost five years

Having been brought up in the English countryside, Darwin was completely unprepared for the magnificence of the rainforest.

Horizons

After reading this book, you may want to find out more about Darwin and his world, or about the evolution of life on earth. At the end of some of the chapters in this book you will find **Horizons** boxes These boxes contain the names of people who were a part of Darwin's world, and of animals that are important in the study of evolution. By looking up these names in the indexes of other reference books, you will discover a great deal more fascinating information.

total distance of more than 60,000 kilometres. The student who had roamed across the British countryside explored remote islands and clambered over the sides of volcanoes. The beetle collector who expected to spend his time among familiar British wildlife was amazed by the variety of exotic plants and animals found in a tropical rainforest.

Everything about the voyage — the sights, sounds, tastes and smells — made a tremendous impression on Darwin. Thousands of questions (and hundreds of possible answers) constantly buzzed in his mind. Many of these he wrote down, but it was only later, back in England, that he was able to sort out his memories and make sense of what he had experienced.

People often think of the voyage of the *Beagle* as Darwin's voyage. However, it must be remembered that the *Beagle* was a survey ship. Darwin was a passenger who went along as an unpaid plant and animal collector.

A voyage of exploration

As an explorer of the physical world, Darwin discovered little that was especially new or startling. But he did develop one of the most important scientific ideas of all time — his theory of evolution. By combining his own observations with the latest scientific thinking, Darwin was able to provide the key to understanding the story of life on earth.

Darwin kept a diary (of day-to-day events) and a journal (for ideas and observations) while on board ship. Later, he wrote an account of the voyage as well as an autobiography (his own life story). As a result, there is a great deal of information available, both about the voyage of the *Beagle* and about what went on in Darwin's mind during the voyage.

The historical background

Birds' eggs (above) and shells (below): illustrations from 19th-century books. As a child, Darwin collected both eggs and shells.

Choosing a career

Charles Darwin was born in Shrewsbury, England in 1809. His father was a doctor, his grandfather had been a doctor, and it was assumed that Charles would become a doctor too. But young Charles was not really interested in medicine. As a child he had started a series of collections of coins, birds' eggs and shells. As a teenager he developed a craze for shooting birds, and wanted nothing more than to be out in the fields with his shotgun. However, in 1825 his father sent him to study medicine at Edinburgh University.

Charles was not a good student. Although he did some studying, he found it very dull and preferred to go walking along the coast, collecting sea animals. At this time, the practice of medicine could be a grim and terrifying experience for both the patient and the doctor. Anaesthetics had not yet been invented, which meant that doctors operated on patients who were fully conscious. As part of his training, Darwin observed such operations in the local hospital. During an operation on a young boy who was screaming with pain, Darwin left the room, unable to watch any longer. After two years at Edinburgh, he realised that he definitely did not want to be a doctor.

His father now decided that Charles should become a clergyman. This was quite an attractive idea to Charles. A Church of England vicar had a fairly comfortable life, and there would be

One of Darwin's favourite pastimes as a young man was to go shooting with his friends.

Christ's College, Cambridge, where
Darwin studied for his university degree

plenty of spare time for shooting and collecting wildlife. In 1828, Darwin went to Cambridge University to study classics (Latin and Greek), mathematics and theology (the philosophy of Christianity). Darwin enjoyed his time at Cambridge and took his studies seriously, although he was hopeless at maths. He began to collect beetles, and became friends with the head of the botany department (plant studies) who was impressed by his enquiring mind.

Darwin passed his exams and in January 1831 he was awarded a university degree. However, he had to complete some additional months of study in order to qualify for the Church. During this time, the botanist introduced him to a professor of geology (the study of rocks). The professor took Darwin on a field trip to collect rock samples and fossils, and Darwin quickly became fascinated by geology. When he returned to the family home in September 1831, he found a very strange letter awaiting him. It was from his friend the botanist.

An unexpected invitation

The letter informed Darwin that the captain of a Royal Navy survey ship wanted an unpaid naturalist to accompany the ship on a round-the-world voyage. The naturalist was to be responsible for collecting specimens of plants, animals, fossils and minerals and sending them back to England. As he read on, Darwin learned that he had been recommended for the post.

For a young man of 22 years, this was a unique opportunity: the chance to see the world and to gain valuable experience. He travelled to London to be interviewed by the ship's captain, who himself was only 26 years old. The two men got on well with each other, although the captain nearly rejected Darwin because of the shape of his nose! As was the fashion at the time, he judged a person's character by his face, and he doubted that anyone with such a nose would have the determination to see the trip through. Despite his nose, Darwin got the job and in December 1831, the survey ship *HMS Beagle* put to sea on a voyage that was to last five years. During the voyage, Darwin saw many things that caused him to think deeply.

Shortly after returning to England, he had an idea. It was a simple idea that made sense of everything that he had seen. However, it was also a very big idea because it challenged the accepted views of the time about life on earth. Darwin was so worried about the controversy that his idea would cause that he told almost no one about it for more than 20 years.

A time of change

In order to understand Darwin's reluctance to publish his idea, it is necessary to look at the world in which he lived. Darwin was born at the beginning of the 19th century which was to be a century of great changes, especially in politics, industry, education and science. Many of these changes affected the lives of ordinary people. For example, at the beginning of the century everybody lit their homes at night with candles and oil lamps. There was no other form of lighting. However, by the end of the century, electric lighting had been introduced in major cities. The replacement of candlelight by electric light took less than 80 years. No wonder that people who lived during the 19th century believed that they lived during an age of progress.

This belief in progress was strongest in Britain, which had become the most powerful nation in the world. Britain itself consisted of four tiny countries (England, Wales, Scotland and

The British Empire in the 19th century (in red), when about one quarter of the world's land surface was ruled from London

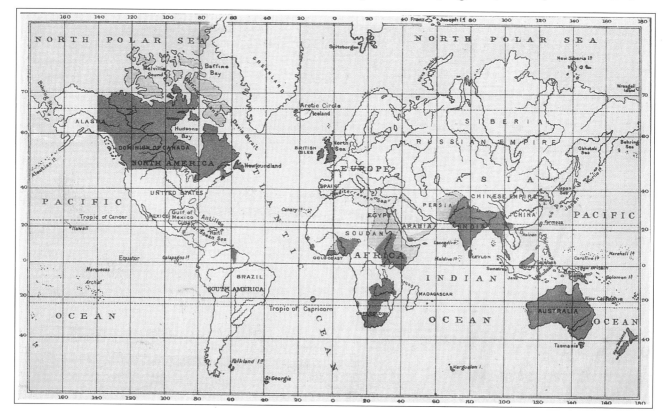

Ireland); but it possessed a vast overseas empire. During the 19th century, the British Empire was to become the largest empire the world had ever seen. By the end of the century the government in London ruled about one quarter of the planet's land surface, and the British Royal Navy controlled the world's seas and oceans. In order to do this, the Royal Navy had to have accurate charts, which is why they sent out survey ships such as *HMS Beagle*.

Industry and commerce

The British Empire was not the only reason that Britain was so powerful. Britain was the first country to experience the Industrial Revolution — the development of engines, machines and large factories. The Industrial Revolution began in Britain in the 18th century, and reached its peak in the 19th century.

Before the 18th century, industry was on a small scale and most things were made by hand. Animals were used for work in the fields, and windmills and waterwheels were used for grinding corn and pumping water. However, towards the end of the 18th century industry in Britain began to change. Water power was used to drive machines such as spinning wheels and looms. New methods of making iron and steel were discovered, and steam power was invented.

During the 19th century, industry changed even more rapidly. By the middle of the century factories had become surprisingly modern, with large steam engines powering dozens of complicated machines. Towns and cities grew in size as people flooded in to work in the new factories. New means of transport, such as the railways, made travel much easier. New methods of

Working conditions were often cramped and noisy in the Industrial Revolution, and machinery was dangerous.

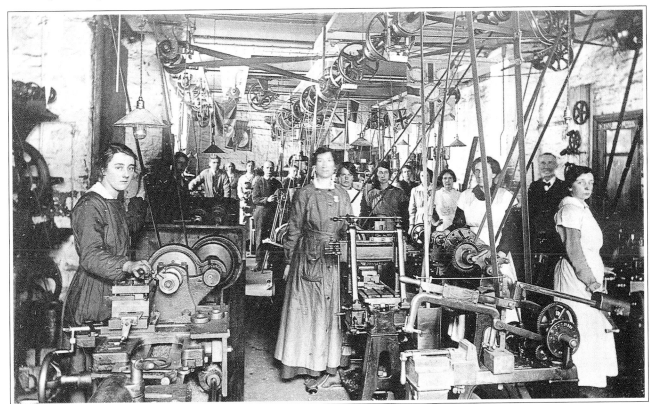

construction using steel girders were used to put up taller buildings and longer bridges. A huge variety of manufactured goods was produced by British factories.

The British Empire and the Industrial Revolution fitted together very well. Many countries in the Empire provided a cheap source of raw materials for British factories. Any manufactured goods that could not be exported to Europe or America could be sold to other countries in the Empire. However, none of this would have been possible without the Royal Navy. The presence of British warships in even the most distant oceans made the seas safe for British merchant ships carrying goods and cargo around the world.

The Great Exhibition of 1851

In 1851, a massive exhibition was held in London. The exhibition was housed in a huge building made of glass and metal (like a giant greenhouse) which became known as the Crystal Palace. The theme of the exhibition was 'progress and invention'. Countries from all over the world were invited to display their latest machines and achievements, but the largest part of the exhibition was devoted to Britain and the British Empire. This was a celebration of progress, and especially of British progress.

The Great Exhibition was a great success, and hundreds of thousands of people flocked to see it. Not all of the exhibits were concerned with industry. Works of art and historical items were also on display. Among the most popular exhibits were several life-size replicas of the newly discovered dinosaurs (see page 35).

The Crystal Palace, where the Great Exhibition of 1851 was held

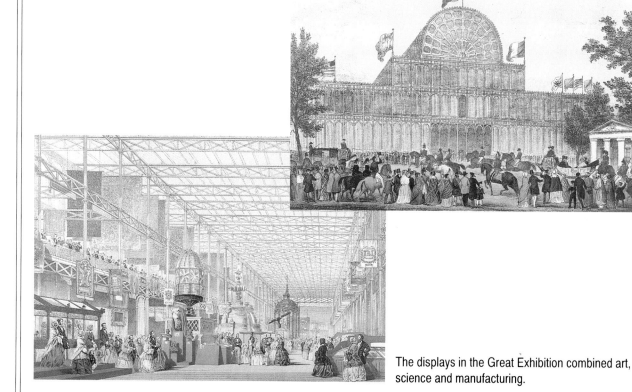

The displays in the Great Exhibition combined art, science and manufacturing.

Revolution and reform

During the French Revolution the women of Paris marched to the Royal Palace to seize the French king.

The 19th century was also a time of political change, especially in Europe. During the second half of the 18th century, the world had been shaken by two great revolutions — the American Revolution (against British rule) and the French Revolution (against rule by a king and aristocracy). The American Revolution was successful, and America became an independent nation; but the French Revolution was eventually defeated and a king was briefly restored to the French throne.

These two revolutions sparked off interest in greater political freedom, and especially in reforms that would give more people a say in government. Many writers took up the ideals of the American and French revolutionaries, and demanded reforms in their own countries. Throughout the 19th century, there was a series of small revolutions in European countries.

Once again, the process of change began in Britain. There was already an elected parliament in Britain, although only the wealthiest people could vote. In 1832, a series of reforms began that gave more people the right to vote. By the end of the century all British men aged 21 years and over could vote in parliamentary elections. British women were not given the vote until 1918.

The Empire, the Royal Navy, the Industrial Revolution and political reform all helped to make British people feel confident,

In 1819 the British Government used troops to disperse demonstrators in Manchester. A number of people were killed, and this became known as the Peterloo Massacre.

Queen Victoria in 1887, when she had already been on the British throne for 50 years

and not a little smug. They felt that they were the most civilised people in the world, and that they lived in the best of all possible countries. This feeling of confidence was increased by the fact that Britain was ruled by the same monarch, Queen Victoria, for more than 60 years (1837-1901). Although the British monarch no longer had any real political power, Queen Victoria was an important figurehead both at home and abroad. She gave people a feeling of stability during a time of huge change. She was also a symbol of established values — especially those of the Church of England.

Church and science

In 19th-century Britain the Church of England had much more influence than it has today. Many people went to church at least once a week and the Sunday sermon was still an important feature of people's lives. Preachers were expected to support the official Church teaching on all subjects. In matters of politics the Church followed the government of the day, and supported its policies. However, in other matters, such as questions of religion and science, the Church had the final say.

At this time, most people were brought up to believe the Bible's version of the story of Creation — that God created the world and everything in it. During the 17th century, an English bishop had even worked out the exact date of the Creation. By adding together the ages of people listed in the Old Testament, he calculated that the world was created at 9am on Sunday

According to the Bible, Noah took two of each type of animal aboard the Ark, so they would survive the Great Flood.

Linnaeus and the classification of species

Carolus Linnaeus (1707-1778) was a Swedish scientist who concentrated on classifying living things, arranging them into related groups. He invented and gave his name to the Linnaean system of classification, which is still used today. Under this system, every plant and animal species has a scientific name consisting of two Latin words. The first word identifies the type of plant or animal, the second word identifies the particular species.

A species consists of all the plants or animals that share the same characteristics and which can interbreed. Plants and animals of different species cannot normally interbreed and produce offspring. Some closely related species, for example horses and donkeys, can breed, in this case producing a mule. But mules are sterile so cannot produce offspring. Mules are therefore not a true species.

A picture of a poppy taken from a 19th-century science book. The plant's scientific (Linnaean) name is shown.

When Darwin was a young man people believed that all the species were exactly the same as when they were created by God. The idea of a species changing its characteristics over time was completely contrary to the accepted view of the world.

23 October 4004BC. In Darwin's day, that date was printed in the Authorised Version of the Bible, and there was no evidence to contradict it.

Fossils were believed to be the remains of creatures that had been killed by the Great Flood (another Bible story). During the 18th century, scientists who studied plants and living creatures concentrated on identifying and classifying the different species. Like most other people, including the young Charles Darwin, they believed that all the species of life in the world had been made by God during the Creation.

Sailing against the wind

The story of Charles Darwin and his theory of evolution is really the story of two voyages. The first voyage, which lasted five years, was his voyage of geographical exploration — to rainforests, mountains and tropical islands. The second voyage was an internal voyage within Darwin's mind. It began with a flash of insight that explained the nature of the evolution of life on earth. However, this second voyage was to last for another 20 years or so. During that time, Darwin collected evidence to support his theory. He also searched within himself for the courage to face the storm of controversy that was bound to follow the publication of his theory. Darwin knew that his theory of evolution contradicted Church teaching, and he sensed that many people would see his theory as an attack on society.

Horizons

You could find out about these famous people who lived at the same time as Charles Darwin: Prince Albert (Queen Victoria's husband); Abraham Lincoln (President of the USA); Karl Marx (political writer); Florence Nightingale (first professional nurse); Charles Dickens (novelist); Tzu Hsi (Dowager Empress of China); David Livingstone (explorer); Simon Bolivar (liberator of South America).

Methods of transport

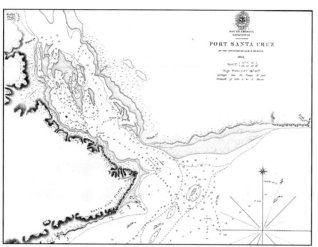

Naval charts show every detail of a coastline.

Surveying the coast

The main reason for the *Beagle*'s voyage was to make a detailed survey of parts of the South American coastline for the Royal Navy. By the 19th century, charts (sea maps) had become extremely accurate and showed every detail of a coastline. Charts were often accompanied by books that listed everything a captain should know about the coastline he was sailing along. Preparing such charts and information was a very slow business because the ship had to keep stopping while measurements were taken.

The surveyors marked the position of prominent landmarks that could be seen from the sea. They visited every port no matter how small, to inspect and record its facilities. Any sandbars or rocks around a harbour entrance were carefully added to the charts, and the rise and fall of the tide was noted. Uninhabited bays and inlets were also investigated in case they could provide shelter from storms, or a supply of fresh water in an emergency.

This slow progress was ideal for Darwin because it gave him plenty of time to go ashore and collect specimens. Sometimes he would leave the *Beagle* for days, or even weeks, and travel overland to rejoin the ship further down the coast.

HMS Beagle

HMS Beagle was a small three-masted ship of the Royal Navy, measuring about 30 metres from end to end. The hull was made

A cross-section of *HMS Beagle*

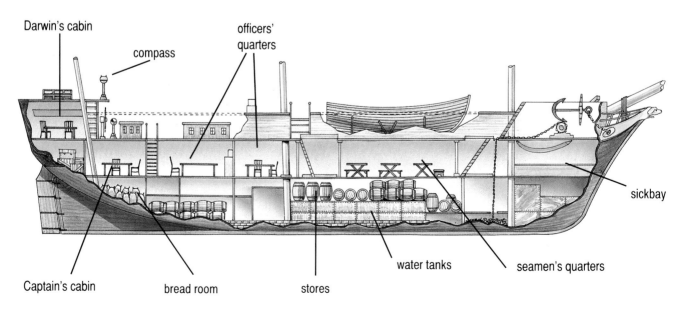

Darwin's cabin

compass

officers' quarters

sickbay

Captain's cabin

bread room

stores

water tanks

seamen's quarters

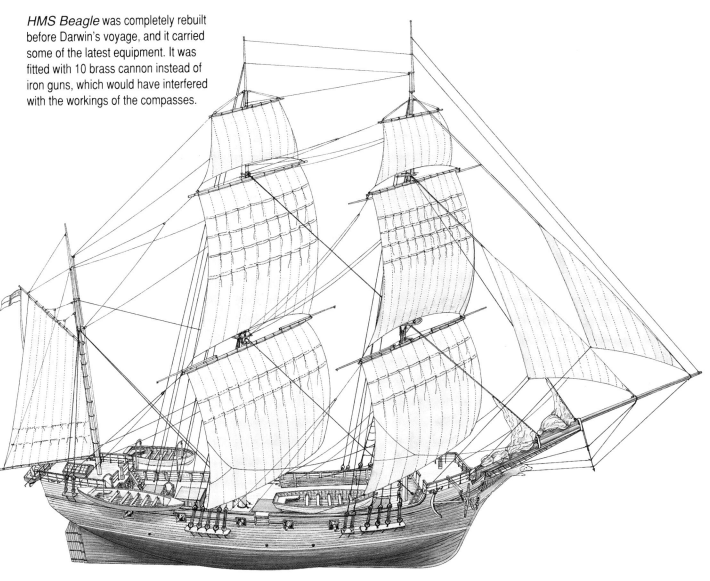

HMS Beagle was completely rebuilt before Darwin's voyage, and it carried some of the latest equipment. It was fitted with 10 brass cannon instead of iron guns, which would have interfered with the workings of the compasses.

The sextant was used at sea by navigators and on land by surveyors to establish correct position.

of wooden planks, and was covered with plates of copper beneath the waterline to prevent marine animals from boring into the wood. The Beagle was not a large ship by the standards of the day. But it was ideal for surveying purposes — large enough to withstand the stormy seas of the South Atlantic, yet small enough to get close inshore. Several small boats were tied to the deck. These were used for ferrying people and supplies, and for exploring rivers.

Altogether, the Beagle carried some 70 officers and men. Most of these were permanent crew: the ship's officers and ordinary seamen (who had to be able to climb high into the rigging), together with carpenters, sailmakers, cooks, and the surgeon (who was both doctor and dentist). However, Darwin was not the only person aboard who played no part in the running of the ship. There was also a party of surveyors, and a ship's artist. The artist drew views of harbours and islands to provide a visual record of the voyage.

Although *HMS Beagle* was on a peaceful mission, the vessel was nevertheless a warship of the Royal Navy, and carried weapons. There were 16 cannons that could be fired broadside from gun-ports just above the waterline. In times of trouble, the guns were manned by specially trained members of the crew who normally had other duties.

All of the permanent crew were accommodated below the main deck. Darwin and the chief surveyor shared a tiny cabin situated over the stern. The cabin was so small that when Darwin lay down, he had to remove the top drawer from a chest in order to make room for his feet. To make matters worse, the rocking motion of the ship gave him terrible seasickness.

Swinging the lead

As well as showing the exact shape of the coastline, and giving details of landmarks and harbours, charts also had to show the depth of the sea. This was especially important close to the coast, where a ship could easily run aground in shallow water. On British charts the depth was measured in fathoms (one fathom equals about 1.8 metres).

Today, the depth of the sea is measured with complicated electronic equipment. In Darwin's day, depth was measured with a long piece of string. A weighted line was lowered from the side of the ship until it touched the sea bed. The line was marked in fathoms with bits of coloured cloth to show how deep the water was.

Measuring depth was often called 'swinging the lead', because the line had a weight made of lead metal. It was a slow process because accurate measurements could only be taken when the ship was moving very slowly.

Some of the birds that Darwin shot and stuffed during his voyage, displayed on a page of his original notes.

Darwin's role

Darwin's task on the voyage was to collect specimens and to send them back for study at the British Museum and other scientific institutions. Darwin was given a supply of specially-designed metal boxes to seal and transport specimens without damaging them. The real scientific work was to be carried out back in Britain, where the specimens could be compared with thousands of others collected in other parts of the world.

Although it may sound simple enough, Darwin's task was certainly not easy. After he had collected a specimen, he had to prepare and preserve it so that it did not rot away before it could be studied. Before he sailed, Darwin took a quick a course in preserving methods (refrigeration was not yet invented).

Insects were the most straightforward to deal with. They were caught by hand, or in a net, and were poisoned in a killing-jar. The best specimens were then placed in small cardboard packets. Reptiles and amphibians, such as snakes and frogs, were also easily trapped. They were usually stored in glass jars of liquid chemical preservative.

Birds were more difficult. The specimen had to be killed without damaging its plumage (feathers). This was usually done by shooting it with very fine lead shot called 'pepper-shot'. The holes made by the shot were too small to be noticeable. The specimen then had to be prepared. The body was cut open and the internal organs were removed. The inside surfaces were smeared with a preservative paste, and the body was stuffed with dry straw and sewn up. Mammals were treated in much the same way.

Darwin soon became very skilful at preparing specimens, and kept very precise records. He carefully labelled each specimen, noting exactly where and when it had been obtained. His work was so good that when he returned to Britain he found that he was already well-known in scientific circles.

Travelling companions

Exotic sights and sounds were not the only influences on Darwin's mind during the voyage. Two of Darwin's travelling companions also played their part in the development of his theory of evolution, because they kept the question of the Creation at the front of his mind. One of them, the ship's captain was present in the flesh. The other was there in spirit only.

At 26, Robert FitzRoy was young to be a captain, but he was an accomplished seaman. He wanted a companion for the voyage; someone he could talk to in order to relieve the boredom of nonstop sailing and surveying. Darwin was to be this companion on the voyage of the *Beagle*. Captain FitzRoy was also using the voyage to take three passengers home. On a previous voyage, FitzRoy had befriended some natives in Tierra del Fuego and had taken them back to England to be educated. The natives were now ready, or so FitzRoy believed, to return to their own people.

Captain FitzRoy was a deeply religious man who believed that every word of the Bible was true. But like many people of this time, he suffered from nagging doubts. He desperately wanted proof that the Church was right, and he secretly hoped that Darwin would discover the site of the Garden of Eden. During the voyage, FitzRoy had an odd relationship with Darwin. At times he would pretend not to be interested in what the naturalist was doing, and would mock the specimens that Darwin brought back. At other times, he would argue fiercely that the specimens proved that the Bible was correct.

Years later, at a meeting where Darwin's theory was being discussed, FitzRoy stood up waving a copy of the Bible and shouted to the audience to believe 'God rather than man'. Later, when he realised that Darwin's theory had been accepted, and depressed by failures in his own life, FitzRoy killed himself.

Charles Lyell was Darwin's other thought-provoking companion on the voyage, although the two men were not to meet until Darwin returned to England. Lyell was one of the new generation of geologists, who were challenging the established views of the 18th century. In 1830, the year before Darwin sailed, Lyell published the first volume of his *Principles of Geology,* and Darwin took a copy with him on the voyage.

In the book, Lyell argued that the earth was

A portrait of Captain FitzRoy later in his career, when he had been promoted to the rank of vice-admiral

Portraits made by Captain FitzRoy of two of the Fuegians, Jeremy Button and Fuegia Basket, during the voyage to take them home

This valley was once V-shaped until a glacier gouged it into a U-shape, thousands of years ago.

much older than the date calculated from the Bible (see page 12). In fact, so many fossils had already been found in different layers of rock that most geologists had already realised this. Lyell then pointed out that since many of the fossils were of creatures that no longer existed, the people who believed in the Creation by God (called Creationists) must be wrong. This too was not a new point, and the Creationists argued that the existence of so many fossils proved that there had been a whole series of Creations. Lyell also argued, that the present landscape on earth (with all its mountains and valleys) was not the result of an act of Creation by God. Instead, the landscape had been shaped by natural processes, such as tide and rainfall, over immense periods of time. This particular thought was to stick in Darwin's mind.

This natural stone arch was slowly eroded by wind and water. It may have taken as long as 100 million years to produce this arch.

The voyage of the *Beagle*

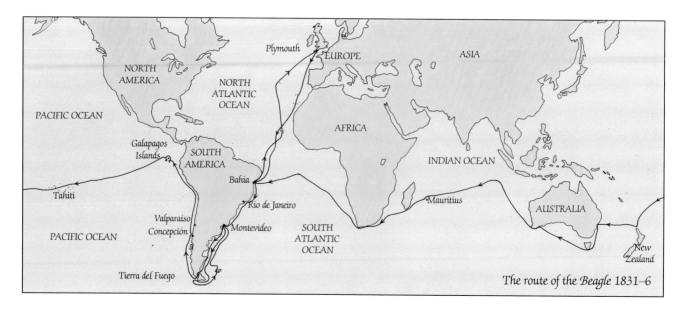

The route of the Beagle 1831–6

First time at sea

On 26th December 1831, *HMS Beagle* sailed from Plymouth, England, and set a course southwest across the Atlantic Ocean. This was Darwin's first (and only) sea voyage, and he was not a natural sailor — in fact he spent most of his time at sea feeling sick. The only place he was comfortable was lying in his hammock, and this presented its own problems. His first letters home are full of complaints about the difficulties of getting in and out of his hammock in the confined space of his cabin.

The European-style cathedral at Bahia, Brazil, Darwin's first port of call in South America

Fortunately, there was not much for Darwin to do during this first stage of the voyage, and he was able to spend his time lying down and reading the latest scientific books. Lyell's book on geology made a particular impression on him (see page 19). After three months at sea Darwin had got used to the constant motion of the ship, and he was able to take part in the traditional celebrations for those crossing the equator for the first time.

The Brazilian rainforest

The *Beagle* arrived at Bahia (Salvador), Brazil, on

28 February 1832. The following day Darwin made his first visit to a tropical forest. He was delighted and astounded. None of his books had prepared him for the magnificence of the Brazilian rainforest. Everything about the forest filled him with wonder — the spectacular plants, their glossy green foliage and bright flowers, and the variety of animal life.

The ship now sailed slowly down the coast to Rio de Janeiro but Darwin spent most of his time ashore, wandering in the forest, observing the wildlife and collecting specimens. He became fascinated by the way that both plants and animals were adapted to their rainforest environment. The idea that living things could adapt to their surroundings was not new. But in the rainforest, where there were so many examples of adaptation, Darwin began to realise that all the various species fitted together like the pieces of a jigsaw picture. However, it was by no means a completely peaceful picture. One day Darwin watched a battle between a spider and a wasp. After a fierce struggle the wasp eventually killed the spider. The battle over, Darwin collected both creatures as specimens.

The Brazilian rainforest is in flower all year round with blooms of every imaginable colour.

This large spider is one of the most savage hunters of the South American rainforest.

Remains in the rock

Leaving Brazil, the *Beagle* sailed southwards along the coast of Argentina to Montevideo. Outside the harbour, the crew sailed into some excitement when another British warship signalled the *Beagle* to load guns and prepare for battle. There had been a local revolution ashore. After hours of confusion, during which an Argentine ship fired a warning shot at the *Beagle*, a party of armed sailors was sent ashore to protect foreign residents.

Further south, the situation was more relaxed, and Darwin was able to spend some time ashore looking for fossils. What was interesting was that while some of the fossils he found were from familiar living species, others were from extinct species. Darwin found large numbers of fossil bones and teeth belonging to several species of extinct mammals. One of these mammals, called *Megatherium*, was a giant sloth that was bigger than a modern-day rhinoceros.

The presence of so many fossils of extinct species made Darwin think carefully about the process of extinction. Was it possible, he wondered, that it was human beings who were responsible for the death of so many species? Or was there some other reason? As it turned out, Darwin was later to show how extinctions were central to the whole process of evolution.

A *Megatherium* skeleton is compared to an average human in this 19th-century illustration.

Geological strata

Geology was to play an important role in Darwin's thinking while he was on board the *Beagle*. It was only by accepting the views of geologists such as Lyell that Darwin was able to develop his theory of evolution.

This 'new' geology claimed that most of the earth's rocks were formed from fine particles of sediment (sand and silt) that were laid down on the beds of rivers, lakes and seas. These rocks are known as sedimentary rocks. The formation of sediments was a continuing process — rivers formed deltas, and harbours often became silted up.

Sedimentary rock is usually found in layers known as strata. It was obvious to geologists that strata were arranged according to time — that rocks in the lower strata had been formed before rocks in the upper strata. The

geologists also knew (from observing rivers and harbours) that it took thousands of years to produce a thickness of even a few metres of sedimentary rock. As some sedimentary rock strata were hundreds of metres thick, geologists calculated that the earth must be millions of years old.

Sedimentary rock is usually found in horizontal layers known as strata.

Primitive islanders

Sailing around the tip of South America, the ship paused for a few days to deliver its young passengers back to their tribe on the island of Tierra del Fuego. Only three of the natives had survived their visit to England — two boys named Jeremy Button and York Minster, and a girl called Fuegia Basket (see page 18). All were dressed in their best European-style clothes for their homecoming and Jeremy was full of chatter. He had learned to speak English, and had also been taught gardening, which FitzRoy thought would be useful.

Darwin had grown quite fond of the Fuegians during the voyage, and he was shocked to see what they were returning to. The native people of Tierra del Fuego existed in a state of primitive savagery. Despite the cold climate, their only clothes were cloaks made of animal skins, and they still used stone tools. They did not have any form of agriculture, but lived on a diet of wild animals, berries and fungi. Some months later, when the *Beagle* returned to Tierra del Fuego, Darwin was surprised at how quickly Jeremy had lost the appearance of European civilisation. He was barely recognisable as the same person, with only a blanket around his waist, and hair over his shoulders.

Before leaving the island, Darwin noted the glaciers flowing down from the land into the chilly waters of the South Atlantic. He knew from reading Lyell that similar rivers of ice had once covered much of North America and Europe, shaping the landscape beneath them as they moved.

The natives of Tierra del Fuego dressed only in animal skins and lived in huts that were little more than crude piles of logs and branches.

A glacier, a river of ice, tumbles slowly into the sea in Beagle Channel (named after Darwin's ship), Tierra del Fuego.

Earthquakes and mountains

The *Beagle* reached the Pacific Ocean and sailed northwards along the coast of Chile. Darwin made a series of expeditions inland to collect specimens and to study the geology of the area. Near Valparaíso, he visited a mine where the local people dug fossil sea shells from the ground for use in making lime. What impressed Darwin was the fact that these sea shells, which had once lived on the sea bed, were now nearly 400 metres above sea level. How had they got there?

At the port of Concepción, the answer came to Darwin in the form of a violent earthquake. The destruction caused by the earthquake was tremendous. Hundreds of buildings collapsed and many people were killed. Smaller earthquakes shook the ruins of the town for days. Afterwards, Darwin noticed that the level of the land around Concepción had been raised by about a metre. Captain FitzRoy reported that some of the offshore islands appeared to have been lifted up by more than five metres. Surely this was the way in which the fossil sea shells had been lifted so high above sea level? However, the process must have taken a very long time.

A few months later, while walking across the Andes Mountains, Darwin found even more dramatic proof of the great age of the earth. On top of a ridge, at a height of more than 4000 metres, he found the fossils of sea creatures. Tremendously excited, he sat down to think. The rock in which the fossils were found had obviously once lain below the sea. Gradually (perhaps through a series of earthquakes) the rock had been lifted up to the top of a mountain. What he saw with his own eyes fitted perfectly with what he had read in Lyell's book. The surface of the earth was slowly but constantly being shaped by natural forces. Darwin wrote in his notebook that for the geologist "...nothing is so unstable as the level of the crust of this earth...".

Tortoise islands

The next stage of the voyage took the *Beagle* to the Galapagos Islands. Named from the Spanish word for tortoise, the Galapagos are small volcanic islands situated in a group about 1000 kilometres west of South America. Darwin arrived just after the

Lush green hillsides on one of the Galapagos Islands. On other islands the landscape is much more arid and bare.

first settlements were established by people from Ecuador. This timing was very important because it gave Darwin the chance to study the islands before their wildlife was affected by the activities of the human settlers.

The most spectacular of the animals on the Galapagos Islands were the giant tortoises, which grew to weigh more than 150 kilograms. They appeared to belong to more than one species,

but Darwin could not sort them out. The governor of the islands remarked that he could tell which island a tortoise came from just by looking at its shell. This was an important clue, but Darwin failed to take notice of it at the time.

The species puzzle

The Galapagos had other strange wildlife including a large lizard called a marine iguana. However Darwin was more interested in the birds, especially the many species of finches. The different species were obviously closely related, but there were important differences between them, particularly the shapes of their beaks. Why was this?

Two closely-related gaint tortoise species of the Galapagos Islands. The differences in the shell markings of these two species is clearly visible.

Darwin realised that explaining the wildlife of the Galapagos presented some tricky problems. All of the species seemed to have relatives in Central and South America, which was the nearest land. Yet none of the species were the same as their mainland relatives. What was even more puzzling was the discovery that each of the Galapagos Islands had its own set of wildlife. How had all the species got there, and why were they different?

Homeward bound

Darwin spent another year aboard the *Beagle*, visiting Tahiti, New Zealand, Australia and Mauritius. While he continued his naturalist duties and collected hundreds more specimens, his mind began to puzzle over the wildlife of the Galapagos, and the bigger question of the force that created species.

On 2nd October 1836, Charles Darwin and the *Beagle* returned to England. Darwin would now start his second great voyage — the voyage in his mind that was to take him to his theory of evolution.

The brightly-coloured marine iguana is found only in the Galapagos Islands.

Darwin's theory of evolution

A coral atoll. Darwin was the first to propose that atolls were found on either rising or sinking land.

Specimens of coral collected by Darwin during the voyage of the *Beagle*

Darwin devoted several years to the study of barnacles.

Respectable success

When Darwin returned to London at the beginning of 1837, he had already earned a reputation as a promising young naturalist. He was introduced to the leading scientists of the day, and presented the Zoological Society with 80 stuffed mammals and 450 birds. Darwin looked forward to a safe, respectable career as a scientist.

He was elected on to the Council of the Geological Society, and began to write a book about the coral reefs of the Pacific. During the last year of the voyage, the reefs had been the things that most interested Darwin. He was puzzled by the fact that many reefs lay just below the surface of the sea, or formed ring-shaped islands, called atolls, that rose only a metre or two above sea level. His own theory (which was correct) was that the coral reefs built up on land that was either slowly sinking beneath the sea, or was slowly being raised up. Here was another strong argument for the earth being considerably older than most people believed.

In 1839, Darwin married his cousin, Emma Wedgwood. In the same year he was made a Fellow of the Royal Society, Britain's most influential scientific organisation, and his first book, an account of his voyage on the *Beagle*, was published. In 1842 his book on coral reefs went on sale, and it received approval from his fellow scientists. This was soon followed by other books and articles about the geology and wildlife he had seen on his travels. In 1846 he began to study barnacles, marine animals that attach themselves to rocks. Over the next eight years he carefully examined more than 10,000 specimens. On the surface, Darwin's life was quiet and respectable. However, below the surface this was not the case at all.

A table in Darwin's study in his country house in Kent. Darwin's microscope can be seen at the front of the table.

A revolutionary idea

Although Darwin was interested in coral reefs and atolls, and in the specimens brought back from the voyage, there was one question that obsessed him when he returned to Britain — the creation of species. He could not bring himself to believe that God had created a separate set of species for each of the Galapagos Islands. The only explanation that made sense was that somehow one species could change into another. In July 1837, Darwin started a secret notebook on 'The Transmutation of Species'. Transmutation means the process of changing into something else, in other words — evolution.

Charles Darwin was not the first person to think of animals evolving. His grandfather, Erasmus Darwin, had a similar idea in the 18th century. And in 1815 the French scientist Jean Baptiste Lamarck had also proposed a theory of evolution, but it was not taken seriously.

Darwin thought that animals did evolve, but he could not work out what it was that made them evolve. He knew that individual species were well adapted to their environment. But he could not see how the process of adaptation happened. The answer came to him suddenly, one autumn morning in 1838, after reading a book by the economist Thomas Malthus.

Malthus and population

Thomas Malthus was not interested in wildlife or evolution. He wrote about economics and politics. At the time of the French Revolution there had been a lot of discussion about improving the conditions in which people lived and worked. This was an attractive idea because it was linked to the idea of progress which was just becoming fashionable (see page 8). However,

Malthus did not believe that it was possible to improve social conditions. In 1798, he published a book called *An Essay on the Principles of Population* to explain his views. In his book, Malthus argued that the world's supply of food could not keep up with the increase in the human population.

For example, if each married couple had four children who each went on to have four children, and so on, then the human population of the world would double every 25 years or so. Even with all the improvements in agriculture, the supply of food could not be doubled in so short a time. When there was not enough food to go round, there was bound to be competition for the food that was available. Some people would be more successful in this competition than others. Therefore it was natural that some people should go hungry, and that some should starve. Malthus argued that starvation was a natural force which prevented the population from growing too large.

A flash of insight

Darwin was not really interested in economics or improving people's living conditions. But after reading Malthus, he saw how some of the ideas in the book could be applied to animals as well as people. The main idea was that of competition within a species. Scientists already knew that different species competed with each other for the same food. However, the idea of competition between members of the same species had not occurred to them. Darwin realised that this was the key to evolution. Without some form of natural control, any species would soon completely cover the earth with offspring (children). Some species of fish laid millions of eggs at a time, but the oceans were not choked with these fish. Most of them died before they were old enough to reproduce.

Darwin wrote in his secret notebook, "Now I have a theory." But he did not tell anyone about his new ideas. They were too controversial, and he knew that nobody would believe him. Instead he carried on with his scientific work, studying barnacles. He did, however, develop an interest in the work of farmers and people who raised pigeons.

A prize-winning bull. Breeders selected certain animals for breeding in order to produce better meat and milk.

Selective breeding

For centuries, farmers had been improving the quality of their animals through selective breeding. Farmers knew that offspring tend to have similar characteristics to their parents. So if a dairy farmer had one particular cow that produced more milk than the others, then the farmer would select that cow for breeding in the hope that

Fancy breeds of pigeon pictured in an old book. Despite their different appearance, all these birds belong to the same species.

its offspring would also produce more milk. Similarly, a cow that produced less milk would not be allowed to breed. In this way, the dairy farmer slowly improved the quality of his herd. A desirable characteristic in one individual was gradually spread through the whole herd by selective breeding. Pigeon fanciers used the same technique, selecting a particular characteristic, or variation, to breed the colourful and exotic birds that won prizes at pigeon shows.

Darwin thought that it must be the same in nature. The individuals in a species that did survive to reproduce were selected as a result of the death of all the other individuals. The best-adapted individuals in a species would survive. Other members of the species would tend to die before they could reproduce. This meant that the variations that helped the well-adapted individuals to survive were passed on to their offspring. Darwin called this natural selection. Over time, the characteristics of a species changed so much as a result of these variations that it evolved into a new species.

Shocked into publication

Darwin still did not publish his theory. He confided in a few friends, but he felt that his ideas were too controversial to make public. He was also not feeling strong enough for a fight because his health was not good. Since the early 1840s, Darwin had suffered from various complaints. He was often able to work for only four hours a day. His ill-health may have resulted from being bitten by insects in South America, he even recorded the incident in his diary. However, his illness may also have been due to the stress of worrying about his theory.

Darwin knew from the beginning just how important his theory was. If he was right then the Bible was wrong, and so were all his fellow scientists who believed that species could not change. Once he published his theory, he knew that his quiet, respectable life style would come to an end.

In 1858, Darwin received a shock. He was sent a scientific paper by Alfred Wallace, a young British naturalist. Wallace had been working in Southeast Asia when he became ill with malaria. While in a fever, a theory of evolution based on selection came into Wallace's mind. When he recovered he wrote his theory down and sent it to Darwin for an opinion.

Wallace wrote to Darwin because he was a well-known scientist. He knew nothing of Darwin's own theory, and Darwin knew nothing of Wallace's work. Eventually, it was agreed that Darwin should be allowed to publish his theory because he thought of it first.

In November 1859, Darwin published *On the Origin of Species by Means of Natural Selection*. The first edition of 1250 copies sold out on the first day.

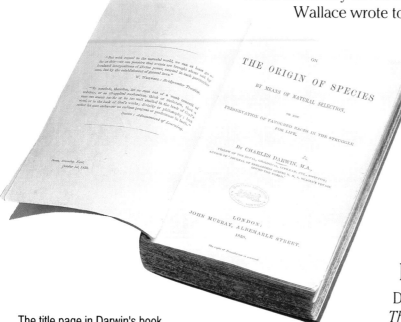

The title page in Darwin's book, one of the most famous and controversial books ever published

Darwin's theory of evolution

Darwin's book, usually called simply *The Origin of Species*, was very detailed. Darwin knew that there would be opposition to his ideas, so he made sure that he included evidence to support all of his statements. He used evidence from geology and fossils, as well as examples from zoology and botany. Darwin's theory of evolution said that the earth was very old and that life had not been created, it had evolved. Modern animals had evolved from more primitive ancestors. Evolution took place as one species gradually turned into another, and this process was governed by natural selection.

Although offspring resembled their parents, there were constant natural variations. Individuals that were born with desirable variations tended to survive to reproduce, and so those

None of these kittens have exactly the same markings as their mother. Nature is continually producing variation.

variations spread through the whole species. All the individuals that did not have this desirable variation were naturally selected for an early death, so that the others could survive. This was how species became adapted to their environment. But, as Darwin knew from experience (see pages 23-4), the environment is constantly changing.

It was the constantly changing environment that caused the continual process of evolution. It was only those species that could adapt quickly to change that stood any chance of survival. This meant that the characteristics of a species also changed. Gradually, a species became so different from its ancestors that it formed a new species — it evolved.

A storm unleashed

As Darwin had expected, the publication of his theory caused an outcry. The Church was horrified by Darwin's theory. Many of the reviews in the newspapers were little more than a string of insults. Cartoons in the newspapers also ridiculed Darwin's ideas.

Darwin did gain some supporters. The scientist Thomas Huxley read *The Origin of Species,* and then said that he felt stupid for not having thought of the theory himself. A few other scientists also became early converts to Darwinism (as his theory became known). At a public meeting in Oxford in June 1860, Huxley defended Darwinism. At the meeting the Bishop of Oxford attacked *The Origin of Species* in a long and boring speech. Huxley responded wittily and then spoke so persuasively that by the end of the meeting there was no doubt that he had won his audience over. There was tremendous excitement, the meeting broke up in disarray, and Captain FitzRoy made a last appearance in Darwin's life, shouting and waving his Bible.

News of the Oxford meeting spread quickly. Many people wanted to read this new theory for themselves, and thousands more copies of Darwin's book were printed. In one of these later editions, Darwin first used the phrase 'survival of the fittest'. These words were suggested by someone else, but he liked the phrase so he included it. Since then, this phrase has been used to sum up the twin ideas of adaptation and natural selection which lie at the heart of Darwin's theory of evolution.

By the mid 1860s, many people had come to accept Darwinism, including a large number of scientists. One of the main attractions of the theory was that it explained things in a completely scientific fashion. For instance, the theory of evolution fitted perfectly with the Linnaean classification of species. The so-called 'higher' species (for example, mammals and birds) had evolved from more primitive ancestors such as reptiles and amphibians.

However, accepting Darwin's theory also meant accepting the idea that humans, too, had evolved. Some people could not bring themselves to accept this simple scientific truth, and remained opposed to Darwinism.

Horizons

These are the names of some other 19th-century scientists, together with the dates of the discoveries and inventions that made them famous: Richard Trevithick (1804, steam locomotive); Michael Faraday (1831, electric generator); Louis Daguerre and William Fox Talbot (1839, photography); Alexander Bell (1876, telephone); Thomas Edison (1879, electric light bulb); Gottlieb Daimler (1885, petrol engine); Gugliemo Marconi (1894, radio communication); Marie Curie (1898, discovered radium).

Evolution in action

The remains of a volcano in the Galapagos Islands. The volcanic cone is composed of black lava rock.

Galapagos explained

Darwin's theory of evolution explained the 'tricky problems' of the Galapagos Islands. In fact, the islands were a perfect natural laboratory for the study of evolution because of their extreme youth and isolation.

The Galapagos are volcanic islands. They are formed from rocks which were pushed up from the sea bed by erupting volcanoes in the quite recent past. The oldest of the islands is no more than five million years old, and the youngest may have been above sea level for less than one million years. Compared to the age of the earth, which is about 4500 million years old, the Galapagos Islands are very young indeed.

Darwin noted that the species of animals on the Galapagos Islands were most closely related to those of Central and South America. Therefore, it was likely that their ancestors came from the mainland. But how had they travelled across 1000 kilometres of open sea? Plant seeds could have been carried by the winds and ocean currents. Insects and birds could also have been blown out to sea. But what about the tortoises? The probable answer to this problem has now been discovered.

Scientists have seen huge mats of vegetation, up to a kilometre across, floating down South American rivers. These mats are solid enough to carry quite large animals. The mats are often washed out to sea, where they remain afloat for several months. It seems likely that the ancestors of many Galapagos species were passengers on similar mats, which were washed ashore on the islands. Once a species became established on an island it began to adapt to the new environment in which it found itself.

The evolution of species

Plants and animals arrived by chance on each of the Galapagos Islands. However, there was little movement between the islands themselves. Although the Galapagos Islands are quite close together, there are very strong currents in the sea between them. These currents make it difficult to float from one island to another. Therefore, the islands remained isolated from each other as well

An American scientist examining some of the finches that Darwin brought back from the voyage. More than 100 years later Darwin's specimens are still being studied as scientists try to puzzle out the evolution of life on the Galapagos Islands.

as from the mainland. As a result, each island developed a slightly different environment, and the wildlife evolved accordingly.

For example, on one island some newly arrived finches found that the seeds of a particular plant were good to eat. Over the years these finches evolved a beak that was the ideal shape for opening these seeds. Finches on the other islands found different food supplies, and in each case they evolved a different suitable beak. All of the original finches probably belonged to the same South American species, but over the years they evolved into 13 different Galapagos species. The same process, of evolution in isolation, is responsible for the many species of Galapagos tortoise (see page 25).

The key to evolution

The Galapagos Islands are unique. Nevertheless, they provide the key to understanding the general process of evolution.

The landscape of the earth is constantly changing. Day-by-day the rain erodes rocks and soils, and rivers carry sediment to the sea. Over longer periods of time the climate may change — 20,000 years ago a thick sheet of ice covered much of Europe and North America. Over even longer periods of time, the sea bed may be raised to become lofty mountains, and new land may be created by volcanoes.

The changing environment presents living things with many new opportunities.

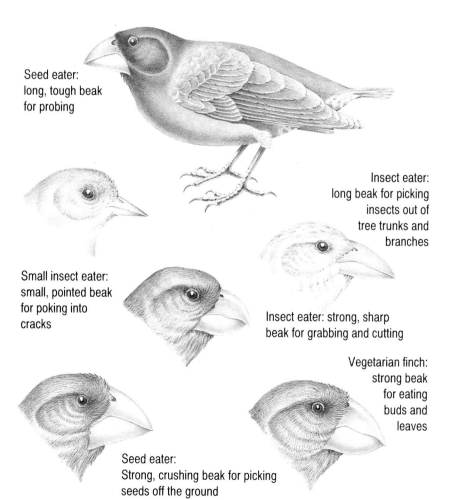

Seed eater: long, tough beak for probing

Insect eater: long beak for picking insects out of tree trunks and branches

Small insect eater: small, pointed beak for poking into cracks

Insect eater: strong, sharp beak for grabbing and cutting

Vegetarian finch: strong beak for eating buds and leaves

Seed eater: Strong, crushing beak for picking seeds off the ground

The different species of finch in the Galapagos each have a slightly different beak which is adapted for eating a certain type of food.

Darwin said that the giraffe's long neck was the result of many generations of adaptation and natural selection.

Evolution is the process by which life takes advantage of these opportunities. For example, an increase in rainfall may make the trees grow taller, raising their branches above the heads of most animals. Those animals with longer necks will be able to reach the branches to feed themselves, and will therefore have a better chance of survival. Eventually a long-necked species will evolve. At the same time, the short-necked species may die out because of lack of food. When a species fails to adapt to the changing environment it becomes extinct. The study of this relationship between living things and their environment is called ecology.

Ecology and evolution

Ecology was not established as a science until long after Darwin's death. Yet, without knowing it, Charles Darwin was one of the first ecologists.

Today, the word ecosystem is used to describe a particular environment and all the plants and animals that live in it. An example of an ecosystem is a forest. Within the ecosystem, the various species are linked by a series of food chains, for example, greenfly eats plant, ladybird eats greenfly, bird eats ladybird, and so on. All of the species in an ecosystem are linked together into a food web. The position of each species in the food web is described as its ecological niche.

In *The Origin of Species* Darwin states that all living things are linked in a 'fragile web'. Elsewhere in the book, he gives a

A food web shows all the feeding relationships between the various plants and animals in a community. An animal's position in a food web is often referred to as its ecological niche.

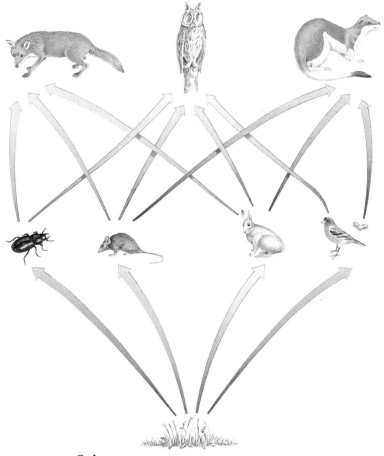

detailed account of a typical ecological relationship between mice and clover plants. He had observed how the amount of clover in the fields was affected by the numbers of mice — the more mice, the less clover. But it was not simply that the mice were eating the clover. In fact, the mice were eating the bumblebees. Without as many bees to fertilise them, the clover plants could not reproduce.

The difference between ecology and evolution is that ecology deals with the relationships between species and their present environment. Evolution traces the development of species over long periods of time during which their environment has changed greatly.

Monster excitement

Darwin's theory of evolution was based on revolutionary ideas, yet it was accepted remarkably quickly, especially by the general public. One reason for the rapid acceptance of his theory was the fact that the public had already been presented with exciting fossils that could not easily be explained. These were not fossil sea shells, nor even fossil giant mammals, but the fossils of huge prehistoric monsters — dinosaurs. Darwin's theory helped to explain the presence of these huge fossil bones.

The first dinosaur remains to be found were discovered in England during the 1820s. Although these first discoveries consisted of only a few bones and teeth, there was enough for scientists to reconstruct what the creatures had looked like. One of the first to be described was a creature more than 12 metres long. It was named *Iguanodon* because it looked a little like a modern iguana. Another was simply named *Megalosaurus*, which means 'big lizard'. In 1841, these ancient animals were added to the Linnaean system of classification (see page 13) under the general heading of *Dinosauria*, which means 'terrible lizards'.

In 1853, a group of 22 scientists ate dinner inside a life-sized model of an *Iguanodon*.

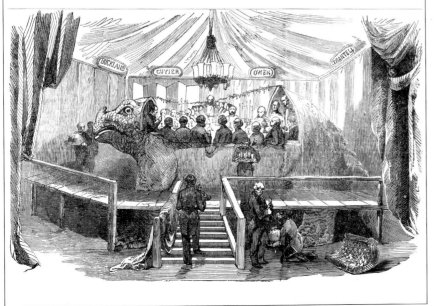

The public was fascinated by these giant creatures, and several replicas were made for the Great Exhibition of 1851 (see page 10). The models were made life size, and were so big that a group of scientists held a dinner party inside one of them. Public interest was also aroused by news of further discoveries in Germany and the United States of America and during the 1870s, hunting for dinosaur bones became big business in America as rival collectors tried to outdo each other.

Human evolution

Darwin's theory was concerned with all life on earth, including human beings. If he was right, it meant that humans were not some special species created in the image of God. Instead they were just evolved animals. Darwin knew that this would be the most shocking of his ideas and he was deliberately vague about human evolution in *The Origin of Species*.

Nevertheless, people who read his book soon realised that, according to Darwin, human beings had evolved from ape-like ancestors and were closely related to monkeys. Many people were both shocked and insulted by this idea. Newspapers and cartoons of the time often made fun of the idea that Darwin's grandfather was a chimpanzee. Slowly, as he was shown to be right about other aspects of evolution, people started to accept the idea that they were not so very different from other animals.

In 1871, Darwin published a new book *The Descent of Man*, which gave a complete account of his view of human evolution. He waited for another storm of outrage, but it never happened. Despite the fact that there was no fossil evidence for human evolution, people were prepared to accept his ideas. One reason for this acceptance was that the idea of human evolution fitted in with the fashionable idea of progress. Human beings could be seen as the most evolved of all animals, situated at the top of the evolutionary tree.

This cartoon makes fun of Darwin's theory that humans descended from ape-like ancestors.

Garden rules

Darwin's theory was accepted because it made sense of all the available evidence; but there was a gap in his theory. Darwin explained the process by which desirable variations spread through a species. However, he could not give a detailed explanation of the way in which these variations are passed from parents to offspring. Darwin died in 1882, without knowing the answer to this problem. In fact, the answer had been discovered even before Darwin wrote *The Origin of Species*. However, this was not widely known until the beginning of the 20th century.

Gregor Mendel was an Austrian monk who taught science in a monastery school. He became interested in plant breeding, and in 1854 he began a series of experiments in the monastery

Strangers in paradise

Darwin was fortunate to visit the Galapagos Islands when he did. The arrival of human settlers at around the same time marked the beginning of the end for some of the islands' wildlife. The settlers brought with them a selection of domestic animals such as goats, sheep, pigs, donkeys, dogs and cats. Some of their descendants now live wild on the islands and these imported animals are damaging the original wildlife.

However, the black rat is now the main threat to the islands' wildlife. It is blamed for the recent extinction of several species of Galapagos rice rat. Black rats also eat large numbers of tortoise eggs. Unless the black rat population is controlled, the Galapagos tortoises may become extinct.

'Piltdown Man'

Many scientists spent years looking for some fossil evidence of human evolution. They particularly wanted to find the so-called 'missing link', — the halfway stage between apes and humans. In 1912, a discovery in England hit the headlines. Some men digging in an English field discovered the remains of a skull that had a combination of both human and ape-like characteristics. They named it 'Piltdown Man' after the place where it was found. For 30 years, 'Piltdown Man' was believed to be the missing link, but unfortunately 'Piltdown Man' turned out to be a clever fake. It had been made by sticking together pieces of human and animal skull. Although 'Piltdown Man' was a disappointment, other genuine human fossils have been discovered, and human evolution can now be traced back over millions of years.

An oil painting showing scientists examining the Piltdown skull shortly after its discovery, when it was still believed to be real.

Horizons

All these animals are important to the study of evolution: duck-billed platypus (primitive egg-laying mammal found only in Australia); lemur (type of monkey found only in Madagascar); peppered moth (moth whose colour has darkened in areas of industrial pollution); whales and dolphins (mammals that have adapted to life in water); coelacanth ('living fossil' fish still found in the ocean depths).

garden. Mendel experimented by breeding between two varieties of garden pea, one tall, the other dwarf (short). By keeping a careful record of his results, Mendel was able to show that some characteristics (for example, tallness) were stronger than others (for example, shortness).

He called the stronger characteristics dominant, and the weaker characteristics recessive. After several years of experiments, Mendel was able to show that the passing on of characteristics, which is called inheritance, follows simple mathematical rules. Mendel published his findings but nobody took any notice. His work only came to light in 1900, when other scientists made the same discovery.

The principles of inheritance are now widely understood. Characteristics are passed from parents to offspring by genes. Offspring receive genes from both parents. For every characteristic, an individual has two genes, one from each parent. Both the genes may be dominant or both recessive, or there may be one of each. In this case, the dominant gene will mask out the recessive gene. An individual will only show a recessive characteristic if it inherits two recessive genes.

Inheritance provided another key to the understanding of evolution. The characteristics of each species are controlled by a set of genes. Usually, those genes are passed from parent to offspring according to mathematical rules, and with predictable results. In this way, the characteristics of a species are preserved.

Occasionally there is a change, or mutation, in one or more of the genes. This mutation produces offspring with slightly different characteristics. If these new characteristics benefit the species, they will be passed on through breeding. Eventually the characteristics of the whole species will change, and the species will have evolved.

After Darwin

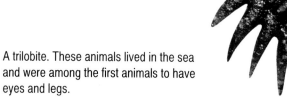

A bacterium magnified 24,000 times. The first living things on earth were like bacteria.

The accepted theory

By the early years of the 20th century, Darwin's theory of evolution had become generally accepted as the explanation for the development of life on earth. The findings of Mendel and of many other scientists added support to Darwin's theory. Geologists found thousands more fossils, and each of these added another piece to the jigsaw picture of evolution. By the middle of this century, scientists were able to give a fairly detailed account of the evolution of life.

A brief history of life on earth

According to the fossil evidence, life on earth began about three billion (3,000,000,000) years ago. The exact origin of life remains a mystery, and probably always will. The most likely explanation is that simple chemical reactions, powered by lightning and sunlight, gradually formed the chemical building-blocks of life. The first living creatures were microscopically small and were rather like today's bacteria. They were made up of a single cell, and they could do little more than eat, grow and reproduce. These primitive creatures lived in sea water.

By about two billion years ago, there were two sorts of these primitive cells. One sort had evolved a method of producing food from sunlight: these were the ancestors of plants. The other sort obtained food by consuming other cells: these were the ancestors of animals. About one billion years ago, the first plants and animals evolved that consisted of more than one cell. These were the ancestors of all the more complicated forms of life that were to evolve later.

Some time around 600 million years ago there was an explosion of life. Although still confined to the sea, living things began to develop more complex characteristics. The first animals with limbs and eyes evolved at this

A trilobite. These animals lived in the sea and were among the first animals to have eyes and legs.

time. By about 400 million years ago, fish had evolved in the sea, and the first plants and animals had begun to establish themselves on land. Scorpions and insects were probably the first types of animal to breathe air and walk on dry land. They were followed by air-breathing amphibians that had evolved from fish. Some of the amphibians later evolved into reptiles.

Approximately 250 million years ago, the earth experienced a massive catastrophe in which 90 per cent of all animal species were wiped out. Afterwards, the dinosaurs became the dominant land animals. The first mammals also appeared at about this time, small rat-like animals that were tiny compared to a dinosaur. Later, some of the dinosaurs evolved into birds.

Sixty-seven million years ago there was another catastrophe, and the dinosaurs became extinct. Since then the surviving animals — mammals, birds, reptiles, amphibians, fish and insects — have evolved into the life forms that we know today.

Scorpions, which originally evolved in the sea, were the first animals to walk and breathe on land, about 400 million years ago.

A dinosaur fossil in America. Gently chipping the fossil out of the surrounding rock is a delicate and time-consuming task.

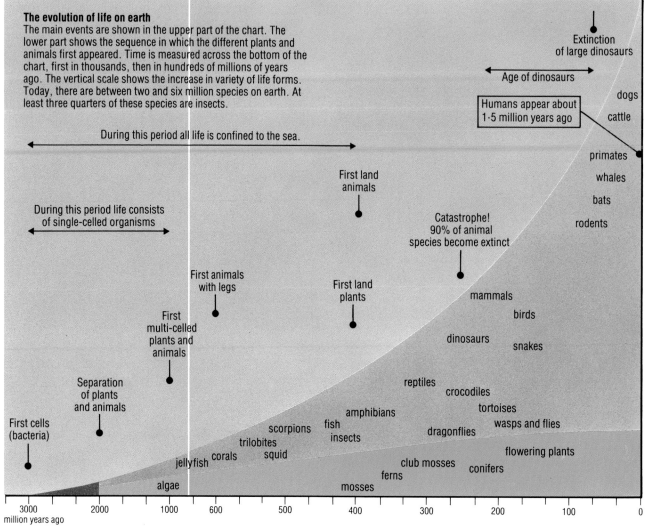

The evolution of life on earth
The main events are shown in the upper part of the chart. The lower part shows the sequence in which the different plants and animals first appeared. Time is measured across the bottom of the chart, first in thousands, then in hundreds of millions of years ago. The vertical scale shows the increase in variety of life forms. Today, there are between two and six million species on earth. At least three quarters of these species are insects.

During this period all life is confined to the sea.

During this period life consists of single-celled organisms

Extinction of large dinosaurs

Age of dinosaurs

Humans appear about 1·5 million years ago

dogs

cattle

primates

whales

bats

rodents

First land animals

Catastrophe! 90% of animal species become extinct

First animals with legs

First land plants

mammals

birds

dinosaurs

snakes

First multi-celled plants and animals

reptiles

crocodiles

Separation of plants and animals

tortoises

amphibians

wasps and flies

First cells (bacteria)

scorpions

fish

insects

dragonflies

trilobites

flowering plants

jellyfish

corals

squid

club mosses

conifers

ferns

algae

mosses

3000   2000   1000   600   500   400   300   200   100   0
million years ago

A branching pattern

Darwin's theory, combined with the evidence of fossils, shows the pattern of evolution to be rather like the branches of a tree. Simple primitive animals evolved into complex modern animals. In the tree-diagram of evolution the most primitive animals are shown at the base of the tree, and the most complex animals such as humans, in the top branches. While this picture is correct, it can give a mistaken impression of evolution.

Placing humans at the top of the evolutionary tree can make it seem that it was somehow 'natural' that humans would evolve as the most advanced life form. In fact, the latest research suggests that human evolution, like the evolution of all living things, happened by chance. There is nothing about our remotest ancestors to suggest that they were any more suited to survival than the species that have become extinct.

It is important to remember that in the continual process of evolution a new species will not always replace an existing one. Each new species is an experiment in life that might or might not be successful. It is natural selection that decides whether it will be the existing species, or the new species, or neither of them, or both, that survives to continue evolving.

The molecule of life

Another piece in the jigsaw picture of evolution was discovered in the 1950s. It came not from the study of fossils, but from observations of living cells. Mendel's work had shown how characteristics were passed from parents to their offspring by genes. But what exactly were genes?

By the beginning of the 1950s scientists had discovered that, during reproduction, genes became arranged into chromosomes. The chromosomes occur in pairs. In humans, there are 46 chromosomes, arranged in 23 pairs. A child receives half its chromosomes from each parent. But what are chromosomes, and genes, made from? The answer lay in a substance known as nucleic acid, normally found in the nucleus of cells.

In 1953 a British scientist, Francis Crick, and an American scientist, James Watson, made an important discovery. They identified the structure of one form of nucleic acid, known as deoxyribonucleic acid (DNA). By the mid-1960s it had been established that DNA did indeed hold the key to inheritance.

Each molecule of DNA contains a series of instructions that control the characteristics of each species. The instructions are held in a chemical code in the DNA. Cells reproduce by dividing and forming two new cells. Some primitive animals also reproduce in this way. Their offspring have identical characteristics to the parent, because the DNA has been copied exactly. However, this is not the case with animals that reproduce through mating, when the offspring receives half its DNA from each parent. As a result it inherits characteristics from both parents. Sometimes there is a variation in the DNA code sequence which produces an altered characteristic. This variation is called a mutation. Such mutations lie at the very heart of evolution. Today, scientists are able to alter some of the characteristics of a species by modifying its DNA in a laboratory. This is known as genetic engineering.

DNA, the molecule of life

The DNA molecule is made up of two long, thin strings arranged alongside each other. The two strings are linked by a series of 'rungs', so that the molecule is rather like a long, thin ladder. In order to fit inside the nucleus of a cell, the DNA molecule is usually wound into a tight double spiral called a double helix.

Each strand of DNA is made up of four basic chemical units. The arrangement of these units forms the code that carries information about characteristics. Each gene is a section of DNA, containing a certain 'message' in the chemical code. In humans, it is estimated that the DNA molecule contains about 10,000 different genes.

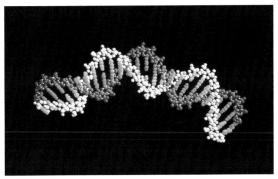

A computer graphic showing part of the DNA molecule. The helical (spiral) shape of this molecule is clearly visible.

Human origins

Mammals first evolved about 250 million years ago, but during the time of the dinosaurs they remained small and rat-like. After the extinction of the dinosaurs, some 67 million years ago, mammals began to evolve into the different forms we know today. Some mammal fossils give clues about the origins of humans. Although the picture is far from complete, it is now possible to outline the 'family history' of the human species by means of fossils.

The oldest remains are those of ape-like creatures that lived between 14 and eight million years ago. These creatures have been named *Ramapithecus* by scientists. They lived in Europe, Asia and Africa. There is then a gap in the fossil record until about four million years ago. During this interval, the evolutionary line branched into two.

One branch evolved into the australopithecines. Although their name means 'southern apes', these creatures were much more like people than apes. There were several species of australopithecines, and the last of them became extinct about one million years ago. The other branch was to evolve into modern humans. There are no fossils until about 2.5 million years ago, when the first remains of *Homo habilis* ('tool-using people') are found. *Homo habilis* had a brain about half the size of a modern human's, and used crude tools made from stone. About 1.5 million years ago *Homo erectus* ('upright people') first appeared. *Homo erectus* people built shelters from animal skins and branches, and organised hunting expeditions. Their brains

A hand axe of the type used by early humans

Wall paintings from Lascaux, southern France. The paintings were made by early humans about 15,000 years ago.

An old woman

Human fossils are rare, but evidence of human origins has been collected from all over the world. Many of the most important discoveries have been made in Kenya, East Africa. In 1974, a half-complete skeleton of a human relative was found there. The skeleton was more than three million years old. It was female, and was nicknamed 'Lucy' by the scientists who studied it.

Lucy was an australopithecine. In life, she was about 1.2 metres tall, and she walked upright. She was only about 20 years old when she died. However, by the standards of her day she was already an old lady.

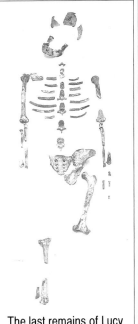

The last remains of Lucy

were about two thirds the size of a modern brain. *Homo erectus* people disappeared about 300,000 years ago.

Modern people, known as *Homo sapiens* ('clever people'), first appeared in Africa about 150,000 years ago. In many ways, these people were identical to modern humans. Another group of people known as *Homo sapiens neanderthalensis* (also known as Neanderthals) appeared in Europe and the Middle East about 100,000 years ago. Neanderthal people had brains bigger than ours, and were the first people to bury their dead. What happened to *Homo sapiens neanderthalensis* is not known, but they became extinct about 35,000 years ago. Since then the world has been populated by modern humans, known scientifically as *Homo sapiens sapiens.*

Darwinism today

Today, more than 100 years after Darwin's death, his theory is still considered to be basically correct. Life on earth evolved through the twin processes of adaptation and natural selection. However, modern research has shown that Darwin was not absolutely correct about everything.

Darwin believed that evolution was a gradual process, with one species slowly turning into another. If he was right, there should have been fossils of the stages in-between one species and another. But there were no such fossils. Darwin thought that this was because they had not yet been discovered.

By the middle of the 20th century, scientists had found many more fossils, and there was a much more complete fossil record. However, the in-between fossils turned out to be quite a surprise. The in-between fossils appeared in very narrow bands of rock strata. This meant that the stages between species had only existed for a very short time. Instead of being a gradual process, as Darwin had believed, evolution is now thought to proceed through a series of sudden 'jumps', separated by long periods when species remain the same. This change to Darwin's theory is known as 'punctuated equilibrium'.

Although this new theory fits the facts better than Darwin's original theory, it does not explain all the fossil evidence. There is still a great deal of scientific research to be done, and the story of evolution is still far from complete.

Horizons

You could find out about these people who have all made discoveries about life on earth: Edward Cope and Othniel C. Marsh (American dinosaur collectors who became deadly rivals); Sir Richard Owen (invented the name 'dinosaur'); Leakey family (discovered fossil remains of primitive humans in Africa); Rosalind Franklin (studied DNA with X-rays); Stephen Jay Gould (published a reinterpretation of the Burgess Shale fossils).

Glossary

adaptation Any characteristic that suits an organism (plant or animal) to its environment. Adaptation is also the process by which such characteristics develop and spread through a species.

amphibian One of a group of animals whose young have gills but which develop lungs as adults. Frogs, toads, newts and salamanders are the main types of amphibian.

ancestor A direct relative who lived in the past.

botany The scientific study of plants.

Creationist Someone who believes that the earth and all natural things were created by a god.

chromosome Tiny rod-like structures made of DNA which can be seen in the nucleus of a cell when the cell divides. Chromosomes normally occur in pairs.

coral reef Underwater structures made up of the stony skeletons of tiny animals called coral polyps which live on the outer surface of the reef.

DNA A short way of writing deoxyribonucleic acid — the molecule that occurs in all living cells. DNA contains coded information about the particular species in which it is found.

ecology The study of the relationships between living things and their environment.

ecosystem A particular environment and the living things found there.

evolution The process by which the characteristics of a species change over time in response to changes in the environment. In general, evolution moves from simple forms of life to more complex ones.

food web A diagram that shows all the feeding relationships (what eats what) between the plants and animals in a particular place.

fossil The term fossil usually refers to some part of a plant or animal that has been preserved in rock. However, tracks and footprints can also be fossils.

gene A sequence of coded information in the DNA molecule that controls a particular characteristic, for example the colour of your eyes.

geology The scientific study of rocks.

mammal One of a group of animals that is warm-blooded and feeds its young on milk produced by the female parent.

molecule The arrangement of atoms which forms the smallest possible unit of a chemical element.

mutation A sudden change in the DNA code which alters a gene.

natural selection The process by which the less well-adapted members of a species die before they can reproduce.

naturalist Someone who studies plants and animals.

nucleus In biology, the nucleus is the small dark area in the centre of a cell which contains the DNA molecule.

reptile One of a group of cold-blooded animals that have scaly skin and lay eggs.

sediment Fine particles of sand and mud that are deposited at the bottom of rivers, lakes and seas.

species A group of plants of animals which have the same characteristics (apart from minor variations) and which can interbreed with each other.

zoology The scientific study of animals.

Index